MW00513366

The complete guide to a low-sodium diet

Peggy B. Sparks

Copyright © 2022 by Peggy B. Sparks

All rights reserved.

No portion of this book may be reproduced in any form without written permission from the publisher or author, except as permitted by U.S. copyright law.

Contents

Introduction

Kidney disease is a widespread condition that affects roughly 10 percent of the world's population

The kidneys are little but mighty bean-shaped organs that are involved in a variety of vital activities. They are in charge of filtering waste, releasing hormones to regulate blood pressure, regulating fluids in the body, generating urine, and a variety of other vital functions

There are several ways in which these important organs can be harmed.

The most frequent risk factors for renal disease are high blood pressure and diabetes. smoking, Obesity, genetics, age and, gender, on the other hand, can all enhance the risk uncontrolled blood sugar and High blood pressure damage blood vessels in the kidneys, limiting their ability to function optimally

When the kidneys fail to function effectively, waste accumulates in the blood, especially waste products from the diet

As a result, persons with the renal illness must adhere to a particular diet known as renal diet.

Chapter 1 What Is Renal Diet

A kidney diet is low in salt, phosphorus, and protein. A renal diet also emphasizes the significance of eating high-quality protein and, in most cases, minimizing fluids. Some people may additionally require potassium and calcium restrictions. Because each person's body is unique, each patient must collaborate with a renal dietitian to develop a diet that is matched to the patient's needs.

The following are some substances that must be monitored in order to support a renal diet:

1.1. Sodium And Its Role in The Body Sodium is a mineral that may be found in various natural foods. Most people consider salt and sodium to be interchangeable. Salt, on the other hand, is a sodium chloride substance. Foods that we consume may include salt or sodium in various ways. Because of the additional salt, processed foods frequently have greater sodium levels.

Sodium is one of the three primary electrolytes in the body (chloride and potassium are the other two). Electrolytes regulate the flow of fluids into and out of the body's tissues and cells. Sodium is involved in: Controlling blood pressure and volume

Balancing how much fluid the body retains or excretes Nerve function and muscle contraction are regulated. Keeping the blood's acid-base balance in check

Keeping Track of Salt Intake

Excess sodium and fluid from the body can be hazardous for patients with renal disease because their kidneys cannot efficiently clear excess salt and fluid. As salt and fluid accumulate in the tissues and circulation, they may result in: heightened thirst

Edema is defined as swelling in the legs, hands, and face. Blood pressure is too high.

Excess fluid in the circulation can overwork your heart, causing it to expand and weaken. Shortness of breath: fluid can accumulate in the lungs, making breathing harder.

Ways To Keep Track of Salt Intake

Read food labels at all times. The amount of sodium in a product is always mentioned. Take note of the serving sizes.

Fresh meats should be used instead than processed meats

Choose fresh fruits and vegetables or canned and frozen products with no added salt. Avoid eating processed meals.

Compare brands and choose goods with the lowest sodium content.

Use spices that do not have "salt" in their name (choose garlic powder to replace garlic salt.) Cook at home without using salt.

The total salt level should be kept at 400 mg each meal and 150 mg every snack.

1.2. Potassium And Its Role in The Body Potassium is a mineral that may be found in many foods and naturally in the body. Potassium helps keep the heartbeat normal, and the muscles operate properly. Potassium is also required for fluid and electrolyte balance in the bloodstream. The kidneys assist in maintaining a healthy level of potassium in the body by excreting excess quantities in the urine.

Keeping A Close Eye on Potassium Intake

When the kidneys fail, they can no longer eliminate extra potassium from the body, causing potassium levels to rise. Hyperkalemia is a condition in which there is an excess of potassium in the blood, which can result in:

Muscle deterioration An erratic heartbeat The pulse is slow.

Attacks on the heart Death

Ways to Keep Track of Potassium Intake

When the kidneys no longer control potassium, a patient must track how much potassium enters the body.

To help keep your potassium levels in check, try the following changes:

Consult a renal dietician about developing an eating plan. Choose fruits and vegetables that are in season.

Limit your consumption of milk and dairy products to 8 oz each day. Avoid potassium-containing salt alternatives and spices.

Take note of the serving size.

Potassium-rich foods should be avoided.

Read the labels on packaged goods and stay away from potassium chloride. Keep a dietary diary.

1.3. Phosphorus And Its Role in The Body

Phosphorus is a mineral that is essential for bone formation and maintenance. Phosphorus also contributes to the growth of connective tissue and organs and the movement of muscles. When phosphorus-containing food is taken and digested, the phosphorus is absorbed by the small intestines and deposited in the bones.

Why should renal patients keep track of their Phosphorus intake?

Normal functioning kidneys may remove extra phosphorus in your blood. When kidney function is impaired, the kidneys cannot eliminate excess phosphorus. Phosphorus levels that are too high might cause calcium to be drawn out of your bones, weakening them. This also causes hazardous calcium deposits in blood vessels, lungs, eyes, and the heart.

Keeping Track of Phosphorus Consumption

Phosphorus may be present in a variety of foods. As a result, individuals with impaired kidney function should consult with a renal dietician to regulate their phosphorus levels.

Tips for keeping phosphorus levels safe:

Learn which foods are low in phosphorus.

Consult your doctor about using phosphate binders at mealtime. At meals and snacks, eat smaller servings of protein-rich foods. Keep a tight eye on the serving size.

Avoid packaged foods with added phosphorus. On ingredient labels, look for phosphorus or terms beginning with "PHOS."

Consume plenty of fresh fruits and vegetables. Keep a dietary diary.

1.4. Protein

Protein is not a concern for kidneys that are in good condition. Normally, protein is consumed, and waste products are produced, which are then filtered by the kidney's nephrons. The waste is then converted into the urine with the aid of extrarenal proteins. On the other hand, damaged kidneys fail to eliminate protein waste, allowing it to build in the blood.

Protein consumption might be difficult for chronic kidney disease patients since the amount varies depending on the stage of the disease. Protein is required for tissue maintenance and other body functions. Thus, it is critical to consume the quantity prescribed by your nephrologist or renal dietitian for your specific stage of illness.

INGREDIENTS

• 12 cup unsalted butter• 1 14 cup sugar• 2 eggs• 2 cups 1% milk• 2 cups all-purpose flour• 2 teaspoons baking powder• 12 teaspoon salt• 2 12 cup fresh blueberries• 2 teaspoons sugar (for topping) (for topping)

CALORIES IN EACH SERVING: 275

9 grams of fat Cholesterol 53mg Saturateci Fat Sg Trans Fat Carbohydrates 44 gs14 Sodium 210 mgs

Sg Dietary Fiber 1.3 g Calcium 108 mg Phosphorus 100 mgsPotassium 121 mg

DIRECTIONS

Step 1sBlend the margarine and sugar in a low-speed mixer until fluffy and creamy.

Step 2sBlend in the eggs one at a time.

Sift the dry ingredients and alternate with the milk in Step 3.

12 cup blueberries, mashed and stirred in by hand Then, by hand, stir in the remaining blueberries.

Step 5sApply vegetable oil to the muffin cups and the pan's surface. In a muffin tin, arrange the muffin cups.

Step 6sStuff each muffin cup full of muffin mixture. Top muffins with sugar.

the seventh step

15

Chapter Two

Moon Pie Stuffing on Chocolate Pancakes

Although it is breakfast, it has a dessert-like flavor. Rich, creamy, and oh-so-chocolatey, this dessert is also high in protein, with 7 grams per serving.

1 serving = 1 chocolate panca ke 1 dozen 4-inch chocolate pancakes

• Chocolate Pancakes:s• 1 cup flours• 3 tablespoo ns sugars• 3 tablespoo ns unsweetened cocoa powders• 12 teaspoo n baking sodas• 1 tablespoo n lemon juice

• 1 egg• 1 cup 2% milk• 2 teaspoons vanilla extract• 2/ 3 cup Body Fortress® vanilla whey pro tein powder

PER SERVING N NUTRITION

Total Fat Calories

9gs17 194 cal

4g fat saturateci Og Cholesterol (Trans Fat): 36 mg Carbohydrates Soclium 121 mg Phosphorus 134mg 22 g protein 7 g 135 mg of potassium Fiber in the Food Supply Calcium 67 mg per gram

DIRECTIONS

Step 1: Prepare the Moon Pie Filling

To make stiff peaks, whisk together cocoa powder and heavy cream.

Step 2sWhisk together the cream cheese, marshmallow cream, and whey protein powder for about a minute, or until thoroughly combined, but not overbeaten. Place in the refrigerator, covered.

Pancakes:

In a large mixing bowl, combine all of the dry ingredients and set aside.

2nd Action

18

Chapter Three

Quiche with beefsteaks

In this delicious mash-up, a cheesesteak meets quiche. This delicious dish will appeal to anyone who enjoys quiche, cheesesteaks, or both. At any time of day, this dish is delicious.

1 serving equals 1/6 of a quiche

12 pound shaved sirloin steak meat, coarsely chopped ped

• 1 cup diced onions • 2 tablespoons canola oil • 12 cup shredded pepper jack cheese • 5 beaten eggs • 1 cup cream • 1" x 9" deep par-cooked prepared piecrust*

CALORIES 527 CALORIES PER SERVING NUTRITION

19 g Saturateci Total Fat Carbohydrates 22 g Protein 22 g 20 g Fat 17 g Trans Fat 1 g Cholesterol 240 mg Sodium 392 mg

Dietary Fiber 1 g Calcium 137 mg Phosphorus 281 mg Potassium 308 mg

DIRECTIONS

Step 1: Coarsely chop the shaved sirloin.

Step 2 In a sauté pan with oil, brown the chopped steak and onions until the meat is done. Allow for a ten-minute cooling period. Jet sit after folding in cheese.

Step 3 Whisk together eggs, cream, and black pepper in a large mixing bowl until well combined.

Step 4 Arrange the steak and cheese mixture on the bottom of the par-cooked piecrust, then pour the egg mixture on top and bake for 30 minutes at 350° F.

Step 5 Turn off the oven and cover the cheesesteak quiche with foil. Allow for a 10-minute cooling period before serving.

TIP: To par-cook the crust, prick it with a fork and bake it for 5-7 minutes at 350° F, being careful not to burn it; par-cooking prevents the shell from becoming soft and wet at the bottom, as well as the crust from bubbling up or sagging.

21

Scrambled Spicy Tofu

This vegan, protein-rich tofu scrambler is a tasty breakfast option thanks to a combination of spices and vegetables. The eggs will be forgotten!

Serves 1 (12 cup) = 2 servings

INGREDIENTS

• 1 tablespoon of extra virgin olive oil

• 1 cup firm tofu (less than 10% calcium) • 1 teaspoon onion powder

• a quarter-teaspoon of garlic powder

1/s teaspoon turmeric • 1 dove garlic, minced

Calories 213 Calories PER SERVING NUTRITION

Total Fat: 13 g Saturated Fat: 2 g Trans Fat: 0 g Cholesterol: 0 mg 24 mg of sodium

Protein 18 g Carbohydrates 10 g

22

Chapter Four

Lunch Recipes

Salad de trois peas au vinaigrette de ginger-lime

It's light and beautiful. This lovely salaci features three types of peas (sugar snap peas, snow peas, and sweet peas), as well as a zesty ginger-lime vinaigrette, for a sophisticated yet simple dish.

6 servings (1 cup = 12 servings)

INGREDIENTS • 1 cup sugar snap peas • 1 cup snow peas • 1 cup fresh or thawed frozen sweet peas • Vinaigrette:

• 1 teaspoon soy sauce, reduced sodium • ¼ cup fresh lime juice

• 1 teaspoon fresh lime zest • 2 teaspoons fresh ginger, chopped • ½ cup canola oil (can substitute grapeseed oil) • 1 tablespoon hot sesame oil

24

• 1 tablespoon sesame seeds

• Optional garnish: freshly cracked coarse black pepper to taste

NUTRITION PER SERVIN G

Calories 225 cal

Tota l Fat 21 g

Saturateci Fat 2g Trans Fat 0g

Cholesterol 0mg

Sodium 70mg

Carbohydrates 6 g Protein 3 g

Phosphorus 40 mg

Potassium 117 mg Dietary Fiber 1.8 g Calcium 46mg

DIRECTIONS

Step 1 Lightly toast the sesame seeds in a hot skillet, tossing them constantly for about 3- 5 minutes.

Step 2 In a large pot of boiling water over high heat, blanch ali 3 types of peas for 2 minutes, drain and then shock them in a bowl of cold water. Transfer to a strainer and drain thoroughly.

25

Chapter Five

Lemon Orzo Spring Salad

It don't mean a thing if your spring salad ain't got that zing! Rev up an orzo salad with lemon zest and Vidalia onions. Add Parmesan cheese and rosemary and savor the flavor.

Serves 4 (1 serving = 1 ½ cup portion)

Ingredients

• ¾ cup or ¼ box orzo pasta • ¼ cup fresh yellow peppers, diced • ¼ cup fresh red peppers, diced • ¼ cup fresh green peppers, diced • ½ cup fresh red or Vidalia onion, diced • 2 cups fresh zucchini, medium-cubed • ¼ cup and 2 tablespoons olive oil • 3 tablespoons fresh lemon juice • 1 teaspoon lemon zest • 3 tablespoons grated Parmesan cheese • 2 tablespoons fresh rosemary, chopped • ½ teaspoon black pepper • ½ teaspoon dried oregano • ½ teaspoon red pepper flakes

Nutrition Per Serving Calories

330 cal Tota! Fat 22g Saturateci Fat 4g Trans Fat Og 27

Cholesterol 3mg Soclium 79mg Carbohydrates 28 g Protein 6g Phosphorus 134mg Potassium 376 mg Dietary Fiber Sg Calcium 67mg

Directions

Step 1 Cook orzo pasta accorcling to box clirections, drain and let sit. (Do not rinse.)

Step 2 Sauté peppers, onions and zucchini on meclium-high heat with 2 tablespoons of oil in large pan until translucent.

Step 3 Mix lemon juice, lemon zest, ¼ cup olive oil, cheese, rosemary, pepper, oregano and red pepper flakes in a large bowl.

Step 4 Add sautéed vegetables and orzo pasta into the large bowl and fold gently until well mixed.

Step 5 Chili or serve at room temperature.

28

Knock-Your-Socks-Off Chicken Broccoli Stromboli

Mix chicken, broccoli, fresh garlic, oregano, basil, red pepper and grated mozzarella.

Then wrap it ali up in yum my pizza dough and bake to perfection.

Serves 4 (1 serving = ¼ of stromboli)

INGREDIENTS • 1 pound store-bought pizza dough (Note: dough can be purchased at some local pizzerias as well as grocery stores) (Note: dough can be purchased at some local pizzerias as well as grocery stores) • 2 cups fresh broccoli florets, blanched • 2 cups diced cooked chicken breast • 1 cup shredded low-salt mozzarella cheese • 1 tablespoon fresh garlic, chopped • 1 tablespoon fresh oregano, chopped • 1 teaspoon crushed red pepper flakes • 2 tablespoons flour • 2 tablespoons olive oil

NUTRITION PER SERVING Calories 522 cal Total Fat 17 g Saturateci Fat Sg Trans Fat Og Cholesterol 75 mg 29

Soclium 607 mg Carbohydrates 52 g Protein 38 g Phosphorus 400mg Potassium 546mg Dietary Fiber 2.9 g Calcium 262mg

DIRECTIONS

Preheat oven to 400° F.

Step 1 Mix chicken, cheese, pepper flakes, broccoli, garlic and oregano in large bowl and set aside.

Step 2 D ust tabletop with flour and roll out dough until you reach an 11" x 14" rectangular shape.

Step 3 Place chicken mixture about 2 inches from the edge of the dough, along the longest side.

Step 4 Roll and pinch the ends and seam until tightly sealed (a fork can be used to crimp edges fora tight seal) (a fork can be used to crimp edges fora tight seal).

Step 5 Brush the top with olive oil and make 3 small slits on the top of 30 the ciough.

Step 6 Bake 8-12 minutes or until golcien brown on lightly oileci baking sheet tray.

Step 7 Remove, let sit for 3-5 minutes, then slice anci serve.

Cool and Crispy Cucumber Salad

Cool, crispy anci easy. Mix sliceci cucumbers with sodium-free Italian dressing anci fresh grounci black pepper, chili anci enjoy!

Serves 4 (1 serving = ½ cup)

INGREDIENTS • 2 cups fresh cucumber (sliceci into ¼-inch slices, peeling is optional) • 2 tablespoons Italian or Caesar salaci dressing • Fresh grounci black pepper to taste

NUTRITION PER SERVING Calories

27 cal Total Fat 2g Saturateci Fat Og Trans Fat Og Cholesterol 0mg Sodium 74mg 31

Chapter Six

Herb-Roasted Chicken Breasts

Marinating overnight with seasoning and olive oil makes for a tender, moist herb-roasted chicken breast every time in this easy dish. Simple never tasted so good!

Serves 4 (1 serving = 4 ounces)

INGREDIENTS • 1 pound boneless, skinless chicken breasts

• 1 medium onion • 1- 2 garlic cloves • 2 tablespoons Mrs. Dash® Garlic and Herb Seasoning Blend

• 1 teaspoon ground black pepper • ¼ cup olive oil

NUTRITION PER SERVIN G Calories 270 cal

Tota l Fat 17 g Saturateci Fat 3g Trans Fat Og Cholesterol 83mg Sodium 53mg Carbohydrates 3g Protein 26g Phosphorus 252mg

33

Potassium 491 mg Dietary Fiber 0.6 g Calcium 17mg

DIRECTIONS

Marinating: Step 1 Chop onion and garlic and place in a bowl. Add Mrs. Dash Seasoning, ground pepper and olive oil.

Step 2 Add chicken breasts to the marinade, cover it, then refrigerate for at least 4 hours or overnight.

Baking: Step 1 Preheat the oven to 350°F.

Step 2 Cover a baking sheet with foil, place the marinateci chicken breasts on the pan.

Step 3 Pour the remaining marinade over the chicken and bake at 350°F for 20 minutes.

Step 4 Broil an additional 5 rninutes for browning.

34

Dinner Slow-Cooked Lemon Chicken

Light and lemony, this slow-cooker chicken recipe reguires little prep and minimal ingredients to make moist, tender chicken breasts. A perfect slow-cooker meal anytime, it's especially nice for spring and summer.

Serves 4 (1 serving = 4 ounces)

INGREDIENTS • 1 teaspoon dried oregano • ¼ teaspoon ground black pepper • 2 tablespoo ns butter, unsalted • 1 pound chicken breast, bonel ess, skinless

• ¼ cup chicken broth, low sodium • ¼ cup water • 1 tablespoon lemon juice • 2 cloves garlic, rninced • 1 teaspoon fresh basil, chopp ed

NUTRITION PER SERVING

Total Fat Calories

197 cal 9g

Saturateci Fat 5 g 35

Trans Fat Og Cholesterol 99mg Sodium 57mg Carbohydrates 1 g Protein 26g Phosphorus 251 mg Potassium 412 mg Dietary Fiber 0.3 g Calcium 20mg

DIRECTIONS

Step 1 Combine oregano and ground black pepper in a small bowl. Rub mixture on the chicken.

Step 2 Melt the butter in a medium-sized skillet over medium heat. Brown the chicken in the melted butter and then transfer the chicken to the slow cooker.

Step 3 Place chicken broth, water, lemon juice and garlic in the skillet. Bring it to a boil so it loosens the browned bits from the skillet. Pour over the chicken.

Step 4 Cover, set slow cooker on high for 2½ hours or low for 5 hours.

36

Chapter Seven

Smothered Pork Chops and Sautéed Greens

Southern comfort for the palate: crispy pan-frieci pork chops, smothereci with sautéeci onions, pepper, paprika, garlic anci sc allions anci se rveci with a sicie of sautéeci collarci greens .

Serves 6 (1 serving = 1 pork chop, 1/ 6 sautéeci gree ns)

INGREDIEN TS • Smothereci Pork Chops:

• 6 pork loin chops ("natural" center cut, bone-in) • 1 tablespoon black pepper • 2 teaspoons paprika

• 2 teaspoons granulateci onio n powcier • 2 teaspoons granulateci garlic powcier • 1 cup anci 2 tablespoons flour • ½ cup canola oil • 2 cups low-sociium beef sto ck • 1 ½ cups fresh onions, sliceci • ½ cup fresh scallions, sliceci on the bias

•

Sautéeci G reens: • 8 cups fresh collarci greens, choppeci anci blancheci • 2 tablespoons olive oil • 1 tablespoon unsalteci butter

• ¼ cup onions, finely diceci • 1 tab lespoon fresh garlic, choppe ci • 1 teaspoon crusheci reci pepper flakes • 1 teaspoon black pepper

38

• 1 teaspoon vinegar (optional)

NUTRITION PER SERVING

Calories Total Fat

464 cal 28 g

Saturateci Fat Sg Trans Fat 0g Cholesterol 71 mg Sodium 108 mg Carbohydrates 26 g Protein 27 g Phosphorus 289mg Potassium 604mg Dietary Fiber 1.3 g Calcium 56mg

DIRECTIONS

Preheat oven to 350° F.

Pork Chops: Step 1

Mix black pepper, paprika, onion powder and garlic powder together. Use half of rnixture to season both sides of the pork chops and mix the other half with 1 cup flour.

Step 2 39

Reserve 2 tablespoons of flour mix for later.

Step 3 Lightly coat pork chops with seasoned flour.

Step 4 Heat oil in large Dutch oven or oven-ready sauté pan (no rubber handles) on medium-high.

Step 5 Fry pork chops for 2—4 minutes on each side or until desired crispness. Remove from pan and pour off ali but 2 tablespoons of oil.

Step 6 Cook onions until translucent, about 4-6 minutes. Stir in 2 tablespoons of reserved flour and mi."X well with onions for about 1 minute.

Step 7 Slowly, add beef stock and stir until thickened.

Step 8 Return pork chops to pan and coat with sauce. Cover or wrap with foil and cook in oven for at least 30—45 minutes at 350° F.

Step 9 Remove from oven and Jet rest at least 5-10 minutes before servmg.

Sautéed Greens: Step 1

40

Chapter Eight

Pasta with Cheesy Meat Sauce

To blanch greens, add greens to a pot of boiling water for 30 seconds.

Step 2 Strain boiling water off and quickly transfer to ready bowl of ice and water.

Step 3 Let cool, then strain and dry greens and set aside.

Step 4 In large sauté pan on medium-high heat, melt butter and oil together. Add onions and garlic, cook until slightly browned, about 4-6 minutes.

Step 5 Add collard greens and black and red pepper and cook for 5-8 minutes on high heat, stirring constantly.

Step 6 Remove from heat; add vinegar if desired and stir.

41

Pasta with Cheesy Meat Sauce

This pasta and meat sauce recipe is creamy, comforting and full of flavor! Pasta, meat and two luscious cheeses combine to make this savory dish a meal to remember-and crave.

Serves 6 (1 serving = 8 ounces)

INGREDIENTS • ½ box large-shaped pasta • 1 pound ground beef* • ½ cup onions, diced • 1 tablespoon onion flakes • 1 ½ cups beef stock, reduced or no sodium • 1 tablespoon Better Than Bouillon® beef, no salt added • 1 tablespoon tornato sauce, no salt added • ¾ cup monterey or pepper jack cheese, shredded • 8 ounces cream cheese, softened • ½ teaspoon Italian seasoning • ½ teaspoon ground black pepper • 2 tablespoons French's® Worcestershire sauce, reduced sodium

NUTRITION PER SERVING Calories 502 cal

Total Fat 30 g Saturateci Fat 14 g T rans Fat 1 g 42

Cholesterol 99mg Soclium 401 mg Carbohydrates 35 g Protein 23g Phosphorus 278mg Potassium 549mg Dietary Fiber 1.7 g Calcium 107 mg

DIRECTIONS

Step 1 Cook pasta noodles accorcling to the clirections on the box.

Step 2 In a large sauté pan, cook ground beef, onions and onion flakes until the meat is browned.

Step 3 Drain and add stock, bouillon and tornato sauce.

Step 4 Bring to a simmer, stirring occasionally. Stir in cooked pasta, turn off heat, add softened cream cheese, shredded cheese and seasonings (Italian seasoning, black pepper and Worcestershire sauce). Stir pasta rnixture until cheese is melted throughout.

TIP: You can substitute ground turkey for beef.

43

Rice with a hint of herbs

If you're looking for a quick and easy side dish, look no further. This fragrant, tasty, and fluffy rice is made with a combination of aromatic herbs.

6 servings (1 cup = 12 servings)

INGREDIENTS

• 2 tablespoons olive oil • 3 cups cooked rice (do not overcook) • 4- 5 cloves fresh garlic, thinly sliced • 2 tablespoons fresh cilantro, chopped • 2 tablespoons fresh oregano, chopped • 2 tablespoons fresh chives, chopped • 12 teaspoon red pepper flakes

G Calories 134 Calories Total Fat Sg Saturateci NUTRITION PER SERVING G Calories 134 Calories Cholesterol 0 mg Fat 1 g Trans Fat Og 6 mg of sodium

Protein 2g 44 Carbohydrates 21 g

Chapter Nine

Herb-Crusted Crunch

Roast Leg of Lamb with Herb-Crusted Crunch

This leg of lamb comes out tender and juicy after being rubbed with a spice blend to enhance its natural flavor. The most flavorful cut is a bone-in leg.

12 servings (4 oz. per serving)

INGREDIENTS

• 1 4-pound leg of lamb • 3 tablespoons lemon juice • 1 tablespoon curry powder • 2 minced garlic cloves • 12 teaspoon black pepper • 1 cup sliced onions

• 12 c. vermouth (dried)

Calories 292 Calories PER SERVING NUTRITION

Saturateci (total fat): 20 g Og Cholesterol 86mg Fat 9g Trans Fat Phosphorus 232 mg 46 Sodium 157 mg Carbohydrates 2 g Protein 24 g

Chapter Ten

Dietary Fiber

Dietary Fiber O g Calcium 19 mg Potassium 419 mg

DIRECTIONS

Preheat the oven to 400 degrees Fahrenheit (200 degrees Celsius).

Place the leg of lamb in a roasting pan and set it aside. 1 teaspoon lemon juice, squirted on top.

Step 2 Combine the remaining spices and 2 teaspoons lemon juice to make a paste. The lamb should be rubbed with the paste.

Step 3: Roast the lamb for 30 minutes at 400° F.

Step 4 Remove the fat from the pan and add the onions and vermouth.

Step 5 Lower the temperature to 325° F and continue to cook for another 134-2 hours. Frequently baste the leg of lamb Remove from the oven when the internal temperature reaches 145°F and set aside for 3 minutes before serving.

Chapter Eleven

Bread Pudding with a Lot of Berries

What makes this berry-delicious bread pudding so simple to make? Warm spice notes of orange zest, cinnamon, and vanilla combine in this tasty medley of mixed berries.

1 cup portion equals 1 serving

INGREDIENTS

• 6 beaten eggs • 2 cups heavy cream • 8 cups cubed challah bread

12 cup sugar • 2 teaspoons vanilla • 1 tablespoon orange zest • 12 teaspoon cinnamon • Whipped cream • 12-ounce bag of

frozen berry medley, thawed

Calories 392 Calories Total Fat 23 Calories Saturateci Fat 12 Calories Trans Fat 1 Calories 48 Calories 48 Calories 48 Calories 48 Calories 48 Calories 48 Calories 48 Calories 48 Calories 48 Calories 48 Calories 48

189 mg Cholesterol 231 mg Sodium 36 g Protein 9 g Phosphorus 134 mg Carbohydrates 36 g Protein 9 g Dietary Fiber 2.2 g Calcium 65 mg Potassium 172 mg

DIRECTIONS

Preheat the oven to 375 degrees Fahrenheit (190 degrees Celsius).

Step 2 In a large mixing bowl, whisk together the eggs, sugar, cream, orange zest, vanilla, and cinnamon until thoroughly combined.

Step 3 Using your hands, thoroughly combine the bread cubes and fruit.

Step 4: Pour into a buttered or greased baking dish and bake for 35 minutes covered in foil. Make sure to use unsalted butter if you're using it.

Step 5: Remove the foil and continue baking for 15 minutes more.

the sixth step

49

Chapter Twelve

Lemon Bars with a Burst of Sunshine

These glazed lemon bars are bursting with tangy, lemony goodness. Any citrus fan with a sweet tooth should try this.

1 bar = 1 serving

INGREDIENTS\sCrust:

• 2 cups all-purpose flour • 12 cup powdered sugar • 14 cup all-purpose flour • lemon juice (14 cup) 4 eggs, 12 cup sugar, and 14 cup all-purpose flour are used to make the filling.

Glaze:

PER SERVING NUTRIENTS: 2 TBS LEMON JUICE • 1 CUP SIFTED POWDERED SUGAR

Calories from fats

200 calories per 9 gram

Saturateci (5 g)

53 milligrams (mg) of cholesterol Sodium: 27 mg Protein: 2 g Carbohydrates: 0 g Trans fat: 0 g Phosphorus (28 g): 32 mg Potassium (41) milligrams Calcium 9mg 0.3g Fiber in the Food Supply

DIRECTIONS

Crust:

Preheat oven to 350°F.

1. In a large mixing bowl, whisk together the flour, powdered sugar, and 1 cup softened butter. To make a crumbly mixture, combine all of the ingredients in a mixing bowl and combine well Press the dough into the bottom of a 9" x 13" baking dish.

2 Preheat oven to 350°F and bake for 15-20 minutes, or until golden brown.

To make the filling, in a medium mixing bowl, lightly whisk the eggs.

Step 2:

52

Chapter Thirteen

DIRECTIONS CALCIUM

DIRECTIONS CALCIUM 23MGS

Preheat the oven to 350°F and prepare the brownie batter according to the package directions.

Step 2sLine or lightly grease and flour the bottom and sides of a 12-cup muffin tin with a liner. Bake for 25 minutes after adding the brownie mix to the pans.

Step 3sRemove the brownies from the oven and place one piece of rnint candy in the center. Bake for another 5 minutes. Remove the oven from the heat source and turn it off. Allow 5–10 minutes for cooling.

Step 4sServe the brownie cupcakes after removing them from the pan.

Chapter Fourteen

Cream Cheese Sugar Cookies with a Christmas Theme

When you make these classic, easy, and delectable sugar cookies, every day can feel like a holiday. Sprinkle colored sugar on top of simple or playful cookie cutters. Make your own oohs and aahs!

1 cookie equals 48 servings

INGREDIENTSs• 1 cup sugars• 1 cup unsalted softened butters• 3 ounces softened cream cheeses• 1 large egg

• 12 teaspoon salts• 14 teaspoon almond extracts• 12 teaspoon vanilla extracts• 214 cup all-purple flours Colored sugar can be added as a finishing touch.

PER SERVING NUTRITION sCalories: 79

Sg Fat Total Saturateci 0g Trans fat 3g fat 3g fat 3g fat 3g fat 3g fat 3g fat 16 mg cholesterin 33 mg of sodium 9 gs56 gs56 gs 56 gs56 gs56 gs56 g

Protein

Dietary Fiber 0g Calcium 4mg Phosphorus 11 mgsPotassium 11 mg

DIRECTIONS

Step 1sMix sugar, butter, cream cheese, salt, almond extract, vanilla extract, and egg yolk in a large mixing bowl. Make a thorough mixture. Blend in the flour until smooth.

Step 2\sChili cookie dough for 2 hours in the refrigerator. Preheat oven to 350°F.

Step 3\sOn a lightly floured surface, roll out the dough, one third at a time to ¼- inch thickness. Cut into desired shapes with lightly floured cookie cutters .

Step 4\sPlace them 1 inch apart on ungreased cookie sheets. Leave cookies plain, or if desired, brush with slightly beaten egg white and sprinkle with colored sugar.

Step 5\sBake cream cheese cookies for 7-9 minutes or until light golden brown. Let cool completely before serving.

57

Pumpkin Strudel

This toasted strudel is the perfect twist on pumpkin pie, with the pumpkin filling wrapped in crispy phyllo dough. It's sugar and spice and everything nice for a holiday dessert.

Serves 8 (1 serving = 1 slice)

INGREDIENTS\s• 1½ cups canned pumpkin, sodium-free, unsweetened\s• 1/s teaspoon grated nutmeg\s• 1 teaspoon pure vanilla extract\s• 4 tablespoons sugar\s• ½ teaspoon ground cinnamon\s• ½ stick (4 tablespoons) butter, unsalted, melted\s• 12 sheets phyllo dough (follow package directions for defrosting if frozen) (follow package directions for defrosting if frozen) (follow package directions for defrosting if frozen)

NUTRITION PER SERVING\sCalories 180 cal

Sg Fat Total Saturateci Fat 4g Trans Fat Og Cholesterol 16 mg

Sodium 141 mg\sCarbohydrates 25 g Protein 3g\s58

Phosphorus 39 mg Potassium 119 mg Dietary Fiber 2.0 g Calcium 19 mg

DIRECTIONS

Step 1\sPosition the oven rack in the midclle of the oven. Preheat the oven to 375° F.

Step 2\sIn a mecliu m-sized bowl, combine the canned pumpkin, nu tmeg, vanilla extract, 2 tablespoo ns of sugar and ½ tablespoon of cinnamo n until well-mixed.

Step 3\sUsing a pastry brush, coat the bottom of a nonstick medium sheet tray with the melted butter. On a clean work surface, lay down a single sheet of phyllo dough, and brush it with the butter. Then create a stack o f buttered phyllo sheets, brushing every other phyllo sheet with butter. (Be sure to save a little melted butter to brush the top of the rolled filled strudel, so go lightly when brushing in between layers.) Keep remaining phyllo dough sheets covered with plastic wrap until ready for use, so they do not dry ou t.

Step 4\sOnce ali 12 sheets are used, spoon the mixture evenly alo ng one of the long edges of the stack. Roll from the filled end to the unfilled end, making sure the seam-side faces down.

59

Chapter Fifteen

Glaze

601 serving equals 1 bar (serves 24).

INGREDIENTS\sCrust:

• 2 cups all-purpose flour • 12 cup powdered sugar

•

14 cup all-purpose flour • 12 teaspoon cream of tartar • 14 teaspoon baking soda • 14 cup lemon juice Filling: 4 eggs • 12 cup sugar • 14 cup all-purpose flour

Glaze:

2 tablespoons lemon juice • 1 cup powdered sugar, sifted

PER SERVING NUTRIENTS

Total fat calories

9 grams of 200 calories

Fat 5 g 51 Saturateci

Cholesterol: 53mg Trans Fat: 0g Sodium 27mg Protein 2 g Carbohydrates 28 g Phosphorus 32mg 41 milligrams of potassium Calcium 9mg 0.3g Dietary Fiber

DIRECTIONS

Crust:

Preheat the oven to 350 degrees Fahrenheit (180 degrees Celsius).

Step 1 Mix flour, powdered sugar, and 1 cup softened butter in a large mixing bowl. Make a crumbly mixture. In a 9" x 13" baking pan, press the dough into the bottom.

2 Bake for 15-20 minutes, or until lightly browned.

Filling:

1st, lightly whisk the eggs in a medium-sized mixing bowl.

2nd Action

52

Chapter Sixteen

Melted Mint Chocolate Brownies

This quick brownie recipe starts with a mix and includes a molten, minty chocolate surprise in the center. It's fantastic.

12 brownies per serving of 2.5 oz.

INGREDIENTS

• Brownie Mix by Betty Cracker® (one box) (not supreme)

12 Andes® mint chocolates

• For garnish, use powdered sugar, unsweetened or sweetened cocoa powder, or fresh mint sprigs.

NUTRITION

Saturateci (18 g fat) Trans fat 0g fat 4g 32 milligrams of cholesterol Carbohydrates 36 g Protein 3 g Sodium 147 mg potassium 120 mg phosphorus 61 mg phosphorus 61 mg phosphorus 61 mg phosphorus 61 mg phosphorus 61 mg phosphorous 61 mg 0gs54 Fiber in the Diet

Chapter Seventeen

Festive Cream Cheese Sugar Cookies

When you make these classic, easy, and delectable sugar cookies, every day can feel like a holiday. Sprinkle colored sugar on top of simple or playful cookie cutters. Receive imaginative and get oohs a d aahs!

Serves 48 (1 serve Equals 1 cookie)

INGREDIENTS\s• 1 cup sugar\s• 1 cup butter, unsalted, softened\s• 3 ounces cream cheese, softened\s• 1 large egg, separateci

• ½ teaspoon salt\s• ¼ teaspoon almond extract\s• ½ teaspoon vanilla extract\s• 2¼ cups all-purp ose flour\s•

Optional garnish: colored sugar

NUTRITION PER SERVING\sCalories 79 cal

Total Fat Sg Saturateci Fat 3g Trans Fat 0g Cholesterol 16mg Sodium 33mg Carbohydrates 9g\s56

Protein

1 g\sPhosphorus 11 mg\sPotassium 11 mg Dietary Fiber 0g Calcium 4mg

DIRECTIONS

Step 1\sIn a large bowl, combine sugar, butter, cream cheese, salt, almond extract, vanilla extract and egg yo lk. Blend well. Stir in flour until well-blended.

Step 2\sChili cookie dough for 2 hours in the refrigerator. Preheat the oven to 350 degrees Fahrenheit (180 degrees Celsius) (180 degrees Celsius).

Step 3\sOn a lightly floured surface, roll out the dough, one third at a time to ¼- inch thickness. Cut into desired shapes with lightly floured cookie cutters .

Step 4\sPlace them 1 inch apart on ungreased cookie sheets. Leave cookies plain, or if desired, brush with slightly beaten egg white and sprinkle with colored sugar.

Step 5\sBake cream cheese cookies for 7-9 minutes or until light golden brown. Let cool completely before serving.

57

Pumpkin Strudel

This toasted strudel is the perfect twist on pumpkin pie, with the pumpkin filling wrapped in crispy phyllo dough. It's sugar and spice and everything nice for a holiday dessert.

Serves 8 (1 serving = 1 slice)

INGREDIENTS\s• 1½ cups canned pumpkin, sodium-free, unsweetened\s• 1/s teaspoon grated nutmeg\s• 1 teaspoon pure vanilla extract\s• 4 tablespoons sugar\s• ½ teaspoon ground cinnamon\s• ½ stick (4 tablespoons) butter, unsalted, melted\s• 12 sheets phyllo dough (follow package directions for defrosting if frozen) (follow package directions for defrosting if frozen) (follow package directions for defrosting if frozen)

NUTRITION PER SERVING\sCalories 180 cal

Total Fat Sg Saturateci Fat 4g Trans Fat Og Cholesterol 16 mg

Sodium 141 mg\sCarbohydrates 25 g Protein 3g\s58

Phosphorus 39 mg Potassium 119 mg Dietary Fiber 2.0 g
Calcium 19 mg

DIRECTIONS

Step 1\sPosition the oven rack in the midclle of the oven.
Preheat the oven to 375° F.

Step 2\sIn a mecliu m-sized bowl, combine the canned
pumpkin, nu tmeg, vanilla extract, 2 tablespoo ns of sugar
and ½ tablespoon of cinnamo n until well-mixed.

Step 3\sUsing a pastry brush, coat the bottom of a nonstick
medium sheet tray with the melted butter. On a clean work
surface, lay down a single sheet of phyllo dough, and brush it
with the butter. Then create a stack o f buttered phyllo
sheets, brushing every other phyllo sheet with butter. (Be
sure to save a little melted butter to brush the top of the
rolled filled strudel, so go lightly when brushing in between

layers.) Keep remaining phyllo dough sheets covered with plastic wrap until ready for use, so they do not dry ou t.

Step 4\sOnce ali 12 sheets are used, spoon the mixture evenly alo ng one of the long edges of the stack. Roll from the filled end to the unfilled end, making sure the seam-side faces down.

59

CPSIA information can be obtained
at www.ICGtesting.com
Printed in the USA
LVHW060929120322
713213LV00006B/235

9 781804 379240